At the School

Design and Art Direction

Lindaanne Donohoe Design

Illustrations

Penny Dann

Picture Credits

© Robert E. Daemmrich/Tony Stone Images: cover, 10, 18
© Kevin Horan/Tony Stone Images: 3
© Gregg Andersen/Gallery 19: 4, 20, 22, 24
© Phil Martin: 6, 30
© Don & Pat Valenti/Tony Stone Images: 8
© Jim Pickerell/Tony Stone Images: 12
© Lawrence Migdale/Tone Tone Images: 14
© David Young Wolff/Tony Stone Images: 16
© Arthur Tilley/Tony Stone Images: 26
© Terry Vine/Tony Stone Images: 28

● ● ● ● ● ● ● ● ● ● ● ● ● ●

Library of Congress Cataloging-in-Publication Data

Greene, Carol.

At the school / by Carol Greene.
p.   cm.
Summary: Simple text and photos take a tour
of a school and depict the activities
of a typical day there.
ISBN 1-56766-465-2 (lib. bdg. : alk. paper)
1. Schools—Juvenile literature. 2. School day—Juvenile literature.
[1. Schools.]   I. Title.

LB1513.G74   1998   97-37747
372.12'44—dc21   CIP
                                                          AC

At the School

By Carol Greene

The Child's World®, Inc.

TAP! TAP! TAP! BRRRRING!

RUSTLE! RUSTLE!

The principal runs the whole school.

This principal is talking with some students.

BUMP! BUMP!

RATTLE! RATTLE! DING!

The kindergarten room has books,

games, and toys in it.

BEEP!

It has computers too.

This school is for children in kindergarten through fifth grade. It is an elementary school.

CRACKLE! CRACKLE!

This classroom is for older children.

They are learning about maps.

They are learning about planets, too.

As the grades get higher, the children get bigger—and so do the chairs.

TOOTLE! TOOTLE! THWEET!

Some children learn to play instruments

in the music room.

"Oh, say can you see..."

Children learn to sing here too.

The music room is noisy.
But it is a wonderful noise.

This is the library. *SHHH!*
People are reading here.
The library has books to help children
learn about things. And it has books
to read just for fun.

READ! READ! READ!

I like to read about monsters and dinosaurs and trucks and rabbits and . . .

SPLAT! SPLAT! DRIBBLE! DRIBBLE!

These children are painting in the art room.

Children learn about all kinds of art.

The art room must hold many supplies.

Is that a picture of ME?

CLICK! CLICK!

Older children learn how to use a microscope in the science room.

Younger children learn how plants grow.

The science room is full of things to do.

THUMP! THUMP! THUMP! THUD!

Children learn about exercise in the gym.

They learn about games, too.

Gyms need a lot of equipment.

This is where it is stored.

Mats, balls, nets, bats . . . the room is packed.

The cafeteria feeds many children every day.
CLANK! CLANK! CHOP! CHOP! CHOP!
The cooks try to make healthy meals
that taste good, too.

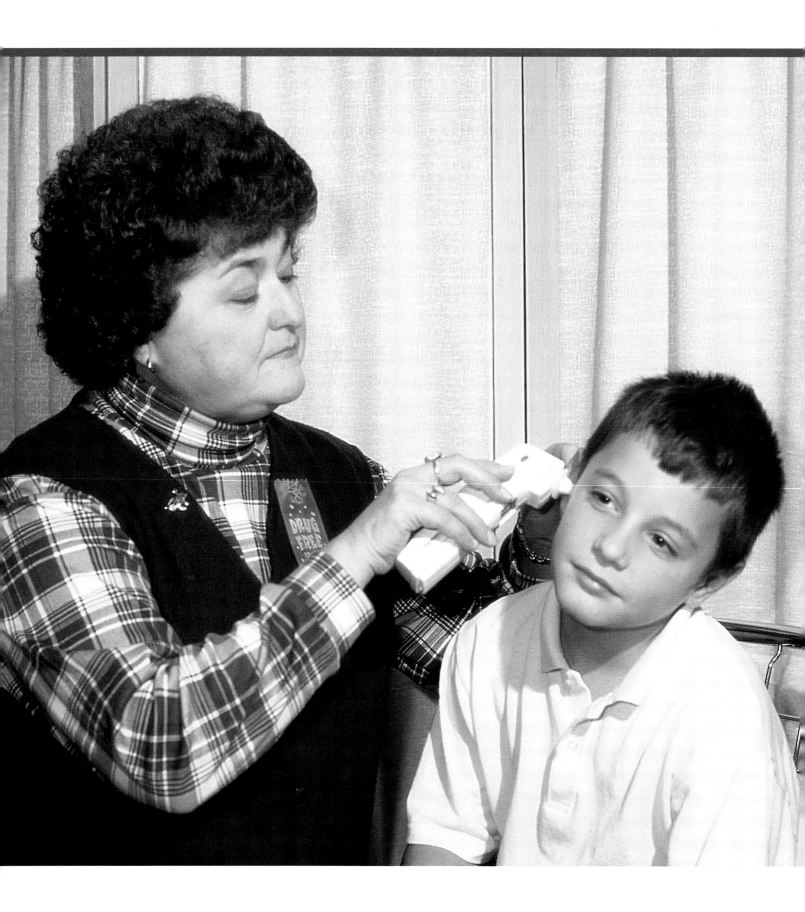

SNIFF! SNIFF! ACHOOO!

Sometimes children get hurt or sick at school.

Then they go to the school nurse.

This boy doesn't feel well.

The nurse checks to see if he has a fever.

The nurse must care for a lot of children every day.

RATTLE! SWISH! BANG!

The janitor has a big job.

He makes sure the school stays clean.

He fixes things that break, too.

This janitor is fixing a small fence outside of the school.

This school has a computer lab.
Here children learn more and more ways
to use the computer.
TAP! TAP! BEEP!

Schools have special little rooms, too.
In this room, a teacher helps a boy with his reading.
In another room, a counselor helps a student
with a problem.

Teachers and counselors really want children to do well and feel happy.

CLATTER! CLATTER!

HA! HA! HA!

Not many children go into this room.

This is the teachers' lounge.

Sometimes teachers eat lunch here.

Sometimes they have meetings.

Sometimes they just need a break

from their students.

Sometimes children need a break from their teachers.

Glossary

cafeteria — a place that cooks and serves food to many people

computer lab — a place where students learn how to use computers

counselor — a person who helps people talk about problems and gives advice

elementary school — a school that has six or eight classes or grades

engineer — a person who cares for the mechanical equipment in a building

instrument — something that makes musical sounds; a tool

kindergarten — the class that goes to school before grade one

library — a place that lends books, magazines, newspapers, videos, and other items

lounge — a room with couches and chairs where teachers can relax

microscope — a device that makes small objects look bigger

nurse — a person trained to do medical work

principal — a person who runs a school

About the Author

Carol Greene has written over 200 books for children. She also likes to read books, make teddy bears, work in her garden, and sing. Ms. Greene lives in Webster Groves, Missouri.